I'm Sad

and Other Tricky Feelings

Clare Hibbert

Illustrated by Simona Dimitri

AMICUS

This title has been published with the co-operation of Cherrytree Books
Amicus Illustrated is published by Amicus
P.O. Box 1329, Mankato, Minnesota 56002

Printed in Mankato, Minnesota, USA by CG Book Printers, a division of
Corporate Graphics

Library of Congress Cataloging-in-Publication Data

Hibbert, Clare, 1970-
I'm sad and other tricky feelings / Clare Hibbert ; illustrated by Simona Dimitri.
    p. cm. – (Feelings)
    Includes index.
    ISBN 978-1-60753-174-6 (library binding)
1. Sadness in children--Juvenile literature. 2. Sadness--Juvenile literature.
3. Emotions in children--Juvenile literature. I. Dimitri, Simona. II. Title.
    BF723.S15H53 2011
    152.4--dc22
                                            2011002243

13-digit ISBN: 978-1-60753-174-6 First Edition 1110987654321
First published in 2010 by Evans Brothers Ltd.
2A Portman Mansions, Chiltern Street, London W1U 6NR, United Kingdom

CONTENTS

Sad

sniff sob

4

sad   jealous   shocked   upset

Jealous

Granny let Archie water the plants. I felt **jealous**.

6

sad

jealous

shocked

upset

7

Shocked

yikes

In my dream, my dog turned into a wolf. I felt **shocked**!

8

sad

jealous

shocked

upset

slobber, slobber

scared   worried   angry   mean   shy

9

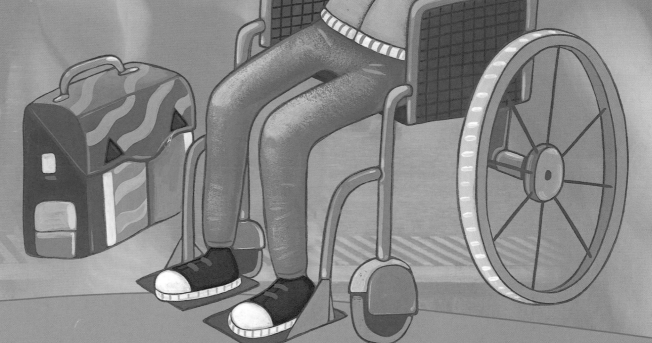

scared

worried

angry

mean

shy

Scared

creak,
creak

12

sad

jealous

shocked

upset

I dreamed about space robots.

I felt **scared**.

tremble tremble

scared · worried · angry · mean · shy

13

Worried

chatter chatter

14

sad jealous shocked upset

OOOps!

SPLASH!

scared

worried

angry

mean

shy

Mean

Waa waa!

18

sad   jealous   shocked   upset

Shy

When I started school, I felt **shy**. I don't any more!

20

sad

jealous

shocked

upset

scared   worried   angry   mean   shy

21

Notes for adults

The **Feelings** series has been designed to support and extend the learning of young children. The books tie in with teaching strategies for reading with children. Find out more from the International Reading Association (www.reading.org), and The National Association for the education of Young Children (www.naeyc.org).

The **Feelings...** series helps to develop children's knowledge, understanding, and skills in key social and emotional aspects of learning, in particular empathy, self-awareness, and social skills. It aims to help children understand, articulate, and manage their feelings.

Titles in the series:
I'm Happy and Other Fun Feelings looks at positive emotions
I'm Sad and Other Tricky Feelings looks at uncomfortable emotions
I'm Tired and Other Body Feelings looks at physical feelings
I'm Busy a Feelings Story explores other familiar feelings

The **Feelings...** books offer the following special features:

1) **matching game**
a border of expressive faces gives readers the chance to hunt out the face that matches the emotion covered on the spread;
2) **fantasy scenes**
since children often explore emotion through stories, dreams and their imaginations, two emotions (in this book, "shocked" and "scared") are presented in a fantasy setting, giving the opportunity to examine intense feelings in the safety of an unreal context.

Making the most of reading time
When reading with younger children, take time to explore the pictures together. Ask children to find, identify, count, or describe different objects. Point out colors and textures. Pause in your reading so that children can ask questions, repeat your words, or even predict the next word. This sort of participation develops early reading skills.

Follow the words with your finger as you read. The main text is in Infant Sassoon, a clear, friendly font designed for children learning to read and write. The thought and speech bubbles and sound effects add fun and give the opportunity to distinguish between levels of communication.

Extend children's learning by using this book as a springboard for discussion and follow-up activities. Here are a few ideas:

Pages 4–5: Sad

Make a story sack themed around losing a favorite toy. You could include *Corduroy* by Don Freeman, *Elmer and the Lost Teddy* by David McKee and *Where's My Teddy?* by Jez Alborough. Encourage children to set up a teddy bears' picnic — they could make pretend food out of play dough.

Pages 6–7: Jealous

Talk about situations in which the children have felt jealous. What made them feel better? Discuss some strategies for joining in, instead of feeling left out.

Pages 8–9: Shocked

If you have a group of children, why not play "What's the time, Mr. Wolf?." One child is Mr Wolf and stands with their back turned. The others stand at the opposite end of the room, yard, or playground. Each time the children call out "What's the time, Mr. Wolf?", the wolf calls out a time between one and 12 o'clock, and the children advance that many steps. But if the wolf calls out "Dinner time!" the children must run back to the start — if the wolf catches one, that child is the new wolf.

Pages 10–11: Upset

Ask children to imagine a best friend moving away. How would they stay in touch? Give each child a sheet of paper so they can "write" a letter to this faraway friend. Divide the paper into eight. In seven of the spaces, write the day of the week, and encourage the children to draw a picture or write a few words to describe what they did on that day. In the last space, they can copy the words "What did *you* do? Love [their name]".

Pages 12–13: Scared

Give each child some cardboard, and markers and ask them to draw the scariest monster imaginable. Help them to cut their picture into six pieces to make a jigsaw puzzle. You can make longer-lasting scary-monster puzzles with a laminating machine.

Pages 14–15: Worried

Provide wooden pegs, glue, and colorful scraps of cloth for making worry dolls. Worry dolls are a tradition in Guatemala. At bedtime, children tell a worry to the doll and place it under their pillow. The idea is that the doll takes care of the worry as the child sleeps (sometimes, parents take away the doll).

Pages 16–17: Angry

How could the girl stop feeling angry? By making an even better picture! Encourage the children to collaborate on a mural, using paints or collage materials, that shows themselves having fun.

Pages 18–19: Mean

Teach some noisy songs that children can sing at home in the bath — far more fun than annoying an older sibling or being mean to a younger one. "Five little ducks" is a good one!

Pages 20–21: Shy

Dressing up and role play are great ways of helping children overcome their shyness. While wearing a costume, they can leave their shy self behind and become someone else — for example, a superhero or an explorer. Animal masks are a useful prop for imaginative, confidence-building play, allowing the children to practice animal moves and make appropriate noises.

Index

Credits

**The publisher would like to thank the following
for permission to reproduce their images:**
Dreamstime: cover and 4–5 (Moth), 18–19 (Cbsva);
iStockphoto: 4 (ivanastar), 6–7 (skhoward), 6 (wwing),
8–9 (AVTG), 8 basket (DNY59), 8 bone (jclegg), 10–11
(assalve), 10 (Ziva_K), 12–13 (Christian Lohman), 12bl
(julos), 12c (paul geor), 14–15 (junxiao), 14 (thepalmer),
16–17 (monkeybusinessimages), 16 (piksel), 18 (jallfree),
20–21 (joelblit), 20 (markross).